T0167688

# *How to Drink Tea*

## An illustrated guide

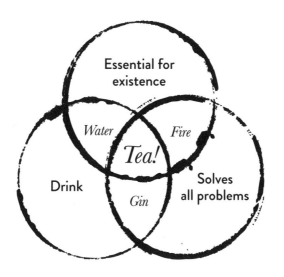

Essential for existence

*Water*

*Fire*

*Tea!*

Drink

*Gin*

Solves all problems

Stephen Wildish

Fancy a brew?

# Contents

# Introduction

What is tea? When was tea? Where is tea?

# *Introduction*

A cuppa, a milky brew, nectar of the gods. Tea is the product of pouring hot water over the leaves from a bush (specifically a tea bush). Black tea is often taken with milk, green tea taken on its own and fruit tea taken to the sink and poured away, because it's disgusting.

A cup of tea contains a heady mix of antioxidants, L-theanine, theophylline and pure liquid nectar of the gods. Hydration and stimulation in one heavenly brew.

If you're not drinking tea are you even alive?

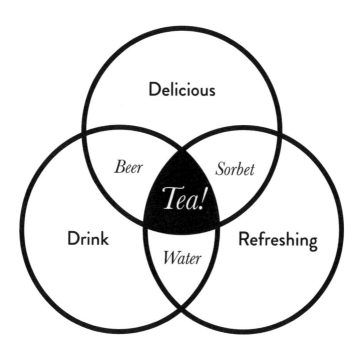

# What is tea?

Leaves are taken from the tea plant (Camellia Sinensis) and prepared by wilting, oxidising and drying. The longer the leaves are oxidised before being dried, the stronger the flavour of the tea.

*Leaves of luxury*

*Buds of bliss*

*Stem of stimulation*

*Camellia sinensis - 'The Heavenly Herb'*

# What isn't tea?

What a silly question. Most things aren't tea. You can't go around putting any old leaves in boiling water and expecting it to result in a delicious brew. If you think you can go to the park and trim some bushes and collect some leaves to make a cup of tea then you're seriously mistaken.

More often than not you're going to kill yourself or at the very least give yourself a chronic case of the trots.

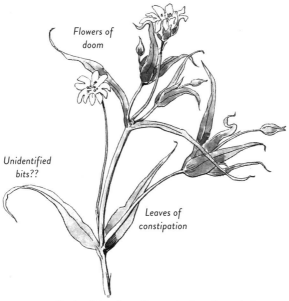

Flowers of doom

Unidentified bits??

Leaves of constipation

*Shrubus Generalius - 'Some twigs from the garden'*

# Should you drink c**fee?

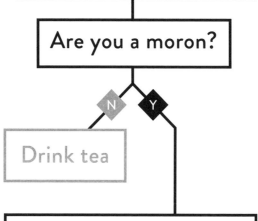

### Are you a moron?

N

Y

### Drink tea

### Sure, fill your boots. You probably would drink it out of a boot as well.

# C**fee

Let's get this out of the way at the top of the book, c**fee
is vile filth and doesn't even approach the delicious
refreshment offered by a beautiful cup of tea.

There are people, confused people, who prefer c**fee over
tea. They think that a drink that is essentially boiled, muddy
toilet water is as good as the 'nectar of the gods'. They are
obviously wrong, deluded individuals and I would hate to
imagine some of their other disastrous life choices. Fools.

**When you asked for tea and they give you c**fee**

# C\*\*FEE
# IS NOT
# MY CUP
# OF TEA

# CAN'T WE ALL JUST GET OOLONG?

# Who drinks tea?

The short answer is everybody.
Next to water it's the most consumed beverage on earth.

In Britain, it's the great social leveller. No matter what class
or age you are, tea is always appropriate. It's drunk in housing
estates by normal people and drunk in country estates by not
quite normal people. Her Majesty the Queen takes tea with
milk and no sugar. Even prisoners are allowed a kettle to make
tea as a basic necessity.

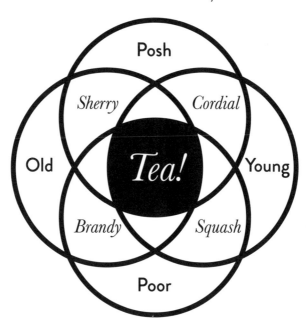

**When you're a queen but also a tea cosy**

# Who invented tea?

It's hard to say who actually invented tea. All we know is that tea was being drunk in China thousands of years ago. Although it was an unrecognisable brew from what we are used to, tea leaves were boiled with other ingredients to form a concentrated liquid used purely as a medicine.

Early tea preparation methods included pounding the leaves into a cake, steaming and then pan frying. Basically, it went through a hell of a time to get to what we now recognise as tea.

**Medieval tea recipes**

# The Classic of Tea

We don't know who invented tea but we do know who first wrote down the recipe. In his book *The Classic of Tea*, written in 760CE, Lu Yu details over 30 implements and pieces needed for the making of a decent cup of tea. Count your lucky stars that all you need now is a kettle and a teaspoon.

**Lu Yu, author of *The Classic of Tea***

# Tea etymology

Most of the world uses one of two sources
as their word for tea: either 'Tea' or 'Cha'.

Like tea, both words originate from China. Traders who
transported tea across the sea mainly spoke the Amoy
dialect, where the word for tea was 'Te', whereas people
who transported tea from mainland China along the silk
road used the Cantonese word for tea, 'Cha'.

What word countries now use reveals
where they first received the tea trade from.

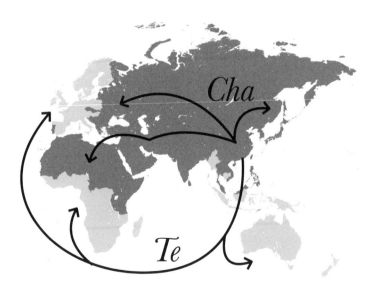

| If it came by sea | |
|---|---|
| **Te** | |
| Language | Name |
| Basque | Tea |
| Dutch | Thee |
| English* | Tea |
| German | Tee |
| Icelandic | Te |
| Irish | Tae |
| Spanish | Té |
| Swedish | Te |

| If it came by land | |
|---|---|
| **Cha** | |
| Language | Name |
| Bengali | Cha |
| English* | Cha |
| Gujarati | Chā |
| Korean | Cha |
| Punjabi | Cha |
| Persian | Chā |
| Portuguese | Chá |
| Tibetan | Ja |

*When tea was introduced to England it came from both sources so the words Tea and Cha are both in use. Although 'char' is normally used by people who are trying too hard.

# ALL PROPER TEA IS THEFT

Karl Marx

# I WOULD RATHER HAVE A CUP OF TEA

Boy George

# Stealing the recipe

For centuries Chinese tea producers had held a monopoly on all the world's tea. Its cultivation and production were a closely guarded secret that the British had tried and failed to replicate. The British thirst for tea was so great that in 1848 botanist Robert Fortune was sent to China to steal the secrets of Chinese tea.

At the time the Chinese interior was a forbidden area for foreigners so quite unbelievably Robert disguised himself as a Chinese merchant and sneaked into the country.

Fortune managed to smuggle seeds and plants out of the country along with all the secrets he needed. He headed directly to create tea plantations in British controlled Darjeeling, India.

The new tea from India began to flood the market and tea shops began to replace those despicable dens of ill repute, 'c**fee houses', that had taken a grip on society. Finally a nation was properly refreshed. The love of tea was cemented into British society.

Robert Fortune, very much NOT a chinese merchant

# The importance of tea

It's not understating it to say that tea is essential to life on earth. It's started wars (American War of Independence) and built empires (British Empire). Add a biscuit in to that mix and you've got yourself a powerful tool.

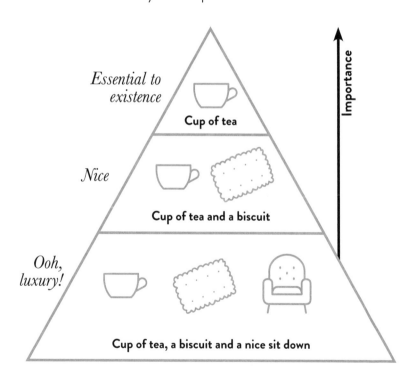

# TEA IS THE ONLY SIMPLE PLEASURE LEFT TO US

Oscar Wilde

# How to brew

The basics of how to get a decent cuppa

# *How to brew*

The rules of how to make the perfect cup of tea are both simple and complex. There are rules that everyone agrees with (tea made in a teapot is the best route) and rules that divide the nation and cause disputes that tear families apart (milk first or last).

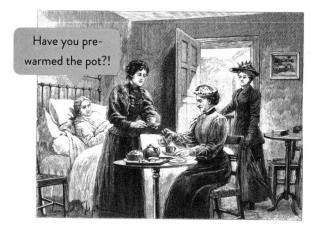

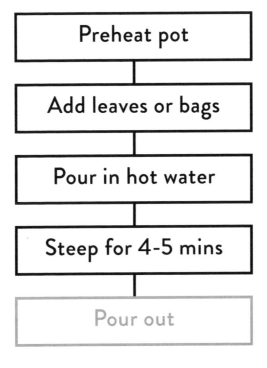

Preheat pot

Add leaves or bags

Pour in hot water

Steep for 4-5 mins

Pour out

# The kettle

A kettle is a vessel designed for the sole purpose of boiling water. It has a handle, lid and spout.

You can use a new fangled electric kettle with beeping buttons that heats the water to 97.75°C and texts you when it is finished. Or you can just use a nice old copper kettle that heats up on your hob. Either way you end up with hot water so it just depends on how much and what sort of a ponce you are.

I loves my kettle, I does

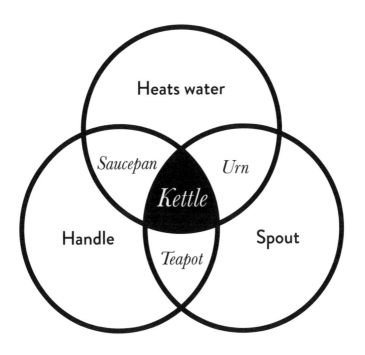

# The teapot

Modern teapots are made from ceramic but originally most teapots were metal. Metal teapots keep everything hotter for longer, but tend to taint the flavour of the brew with, surprise surprise, a metallic tang. Because of the nature of ceramic it doesn't impart any flavour into the tea so leaves it untainted and delicious. When you are finished brewing tea in a teapot you should never clean it with soap but simply swill with warm water. This leaves a residue of tannins in the pot that impart better flavours.

What is and what isn't a teapot can be quite nuanced. Lots of things could be used as teapots if you're creative enough.

### Teapot identification guide

1. This is an urn

2. This is a teapot

3. This is a teapot

4. This is only just a teapot

5. This is a teapot

6. This is a pitcher

7. This is a teapot

8. This is a teapot

9. This is a c**fee pot

10. This is a kettle

11. This is possibly a teapot?

12. This might be a watering can?

13. This is definitely a watering can

# Equipment list

To make a cup of tea all the equipment you will need is a kettle (or a way to heat water) and a cup. But there are many utensils that you can use to make the experience more pleasurable.

**Teaspoon**
For stirring the brew. When stirring your tea try not to bash your teaspoon against the side of the cup. Swirl it gently and place back onto the saucer next to the cup. Leaving a teaspoon in the cup or putting it in your mouth are exceptionally bad manners

**Milk jug**
It's incredibly uncouth to bring a milk bottle to the table. Decant your milk into this and relax into your middle-class life.

**Sugar bowl**
If you must have sugar in tea, then at least keep it covered in a sugar bowl so as not to offend other tea drinkers.

**Sugar tongs**
God forbid you would pick up sugar with your fingers.

**Strainer**
A simple device to separate the tea from the spent tea leaves. You'll forget to use it at least once in your life and pour tea full of leaves into your cup. It will ruin your day.

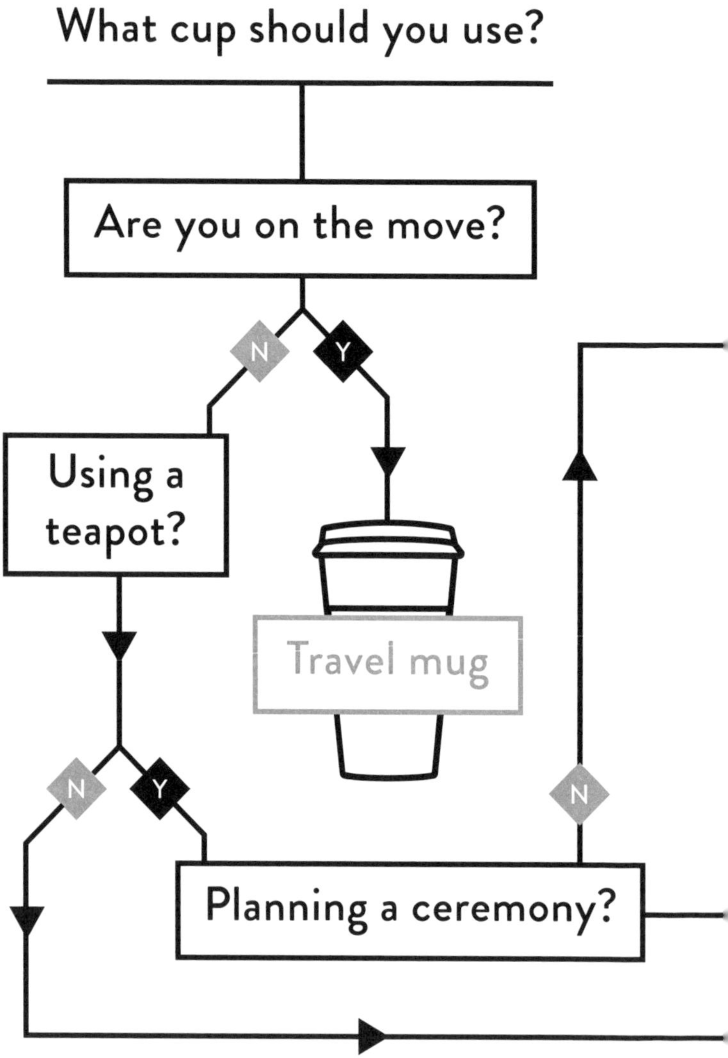

# What cup should you use?

Are you on the move?

N — Y

Using a teapot?

Y →

Travel mug

N

N — Y

Planning a ceremony?

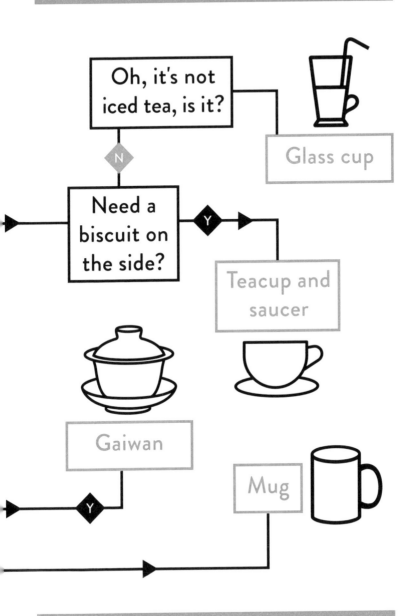

Oh, it's not iced tea, is it?

Glass cup

N

Need a biscuit on the side?

Y

Teacup and saucer

Gaiwan

Y

Mug

# Golden rules

In 1946, when he had much better things to be getting on with, George Orwell penned an essay on the 11 golden rules for making the perfect cup of tea. Most of these have stood the test of time, some are clearly his personal preference and others, like 6 and 9, are outdated. Unless you still have milk bottles with cream on top? Haven't you heard of cholesterol?!

| Rule 1 | Use Indian or Ceylonese tea. |
|---|---|
| Rule 2 | Tea should be made in small quantities. |
| Rule 3 | The pot should be warmed beforehand. |
| Rule 4 | The tea should be strong. |
| Rule 5 | The tea should be put straight into the pot. |
| Rule 6 | Take the teapot to the kettle. |
| Rule 7 | After making the tea, one should stir it. |
| Rule 8 | Drink out of a good breakfast cup. |
| Rule 9 | Pour the cream off the milk before using it. |
| Rule 10 | Pour tea into the cup first. |
| Rule 11 | Tea should be drunk without sugar. |

# Brewing terminology

The process of making tea uses words like 'infusion' and 'steep', but what do they mean and are they interchangeable?

### Infusion

Noun, a drink, remedy, or extract prepared by soaking tea leaves or herbs in liquid.
*'Cecil, make sure my infusion is ready after pilates.'*

### Brew

A noun and a verb, to make tea or the tea itself.
*"Ey up love, want me to brew you a brew?"*

### Steep

Verb, to soak in water to extract flavour.
*'I've left the tea to steep, make sure it doesn't fall off the table as it is too steep.'*

### Stewed

Adjective, bitter, over-brewed. Filth.
*'This tea is stewed, this is the worst thing that has ever happened.'*

# Water

The perfect cup of tea starts with the correct water. Freshly drawn from the tap is ideal (put your pencils away, you comedian, drawn as in turned the tap on). Water straight from the tap has high oxygen levels and this brings out the best tea flavours. If you have filtered water then use that. The purer the water, the better. You wouldn't make tea from a puddle, would you? Well, don't.

Never use reboiled water from a kettle as every time you boil a kettle it knocks some oxygen out of the water and you will end up with a dull cuppa.

### Hard water

Hard water makes darker and richer tea. The limestone in hard water is not a friend to your kettle so you might want to consider a water softener.

### Soft water

Soft water produces a lighter but less flavoursome cup of tea. You're also missing out on some delicious minerals.

### Bottled water

Oh, I'm sorry, I didn't realise millionaires read books about making tea. Using bottled water is a waste of time and money.

### Sparkling water

Don't be ridiculous.

# Boil the water - but let it rest

So you don't scald your leaves (yes, that is a first world problem) make sure you leave the kettle for a minute or two to cool before pouring onto the tea. But won't that make cold tea? If you think that water is cold, why don't you take a lovely big sip straight from the kettle spout? No, of course not, because it will still be around 95 degrees and that is plenty hot enough, even if you do claim to have an 'asbestos mouth'.

Most teas have an ideal temperature to achieve the perfect brew, but in reality you're not going to be measuring water temperatures for each cup you make.

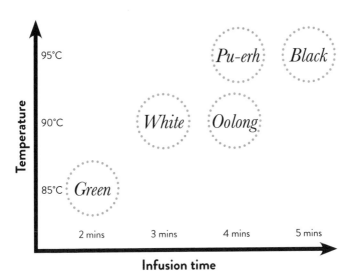

# Milk last

If you are making tea in a cup, to properly brew, it needs the water to be as close to boiling as possible. If you are a simpleton and have milk in the cup you are lowering the temperature of the infusion process and creating an inferior wishy-washy cup of tea.

If you are making tea in a teapot, you will of course not be putting milk into the teapot. You can add the milk to the cup before pouring out without altering the brew. There is a danger that you will 'pour out' before the tea has reached the correct strength and you will have added too much milk. Add milk last and avoid catastrophe.

**When you find out they put milk first**

# Milk first

There are of course some merits to putting milk in first
instead of last when using a teapot. Adding milk last heats
the milk unevenly and this causes the proteins in milk to split.
Enough with the science babble, this is why you might get an
unpleasant skin on the top of your tea. Point conceded, but you
must never put milk in first whilst making in a cup!

# MILK AND TEABAG

# SHOULD NEVER TOUCH

# Making in the cup

Unfortunately, using a teapot isn't always convenient or practical. Then and only then you should make tea in the cup using a teabag. Here are some golden rules for making in the cup:

**Preheat the cup**
Whilst you are waiting for the water to cool slightly and before you add any teabags to the cup you can preheat the cup with a spot of the freshly boiled water.

**Steep properly**
Stick to the timing instructions for the tea you are using. A good rule of thumb is around 4-5 minutes. Any longer and the tea will start to taste bitter. Obviously the longer the steeping time, the stronger the tea. If you like your tea so strong the spoon stands upright then leave it in for longer.

**No squashing the teabag on the side of the cup!**
If you're in a rush then squashing the teabag against the side of the cup can release more flavour into the tea but it can also release more unwanted tannins and bitter flavour profiles. It's better to let the leaves steep naturally than agitate your bag like a fidgeting child.

Learn a thing or two about deferred gratification, you impatient fool!

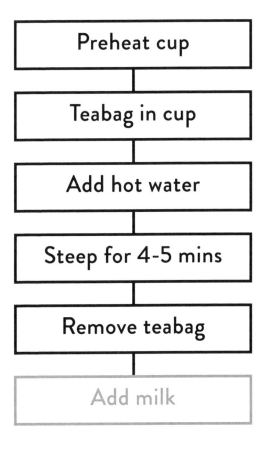

Preheat cup

Teabag in cup

Add hot water

Steep for 4-5 mins

Remove teabag

Add milk

# Teabag shape ranked by poshness

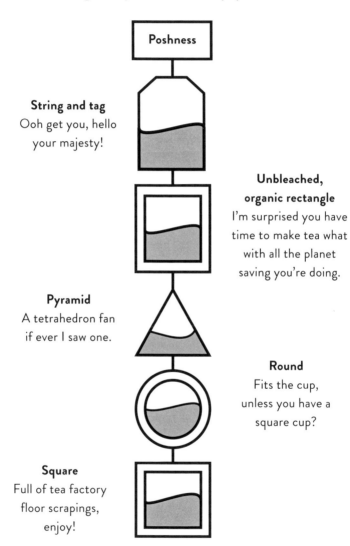

**Poshness**

**String and tag**
Ooh get you, hello
your majesty!

**Unbleached,
organic rectangle**
I'm surprised you have
time to make tea what
with all the planet
saving you're doing.

**Pyramid**
A tetrahedron fan
if ever I saw one.

**Round**
Fits the cup,
unless you have a
square cup?

**Square**
Full of tea factory
floor scrapings,
enjoy!

# Teabags and teabagging

### Teabag types

There are three main shapes of teabag: square, round and pyramid. The various makers of these bags will go to great lengths to tell you their shape gets you a better brew, but if you're an intellectual (you're reading a book about how to make tea, of course you are) then you will know that this is absolute bunkum. Use any shape you like and you will get the same results. The secret to a good cup of tea is not in the shape of the bag.

### Teabagging

When the tea is brewing it can be tempting to swill it around the cup or to dunk it in and out of the cup in a plunging motion. This is called teabagging and it's not acceptable in polite society. The teabag should be left to infuse in the cup and, when ready, removed and disposed of.

# Is it brewed?

This book has been printed in pantone 7411, which is the absolute pinnacle for a cup of tea. You can use the cover as a swatch to test if your tea is correctly brewed.

This is strong!

Just right, good job

So close, you removed your bag early

Milky mess

Nope

You're a disgrace

# Making in the pot

Here we go, the main event. How to make tea in
a proper teapot! Firstly some golden rules:

### Preheat the pot
Before you add any tea to the teapot, swill some of the
freshly boiled water around the pot to warm it. This will
ensure you keep the pot warmer for longer.

### Amount of tea
If you are making tea in a teapot with teabags then add
one teabag per person. If you are using loose leaf tea
then use one teaspoon per person and an extra spoon
for 'the pot'. Nobody knows why, you just do.

### Steep properly
A teapot needs to be left for around 4-5 minutes at
least to fully steep. If you're so inclined now is the time
to swaddle the teapot in an amusing or quaint tea-cosy.

**When 'one for the pot' involves a shovel**

# Being mother

'I'll be mother' needs to be said before pouring out for a group of people. It is polite to pour out a small amount to yourself first to check the quality of the brew, before progressing to others and pouring out for them.

Being mother is all part of the ceremony and the social bonding of taking tea with friends and family, but more importantly it also means that you're in charge of the biscuits!

I'll be mother, Mother

# WORSHIP THE TEAPOT

# AND FORGET TO DRINK THE TEA

Wei Wu Wei

## How not to make tea

As a 'fun' thought experiment to tease yourself you can
imagine how to make the worst cup of tea,
by breaking all the rules we've already discussed:

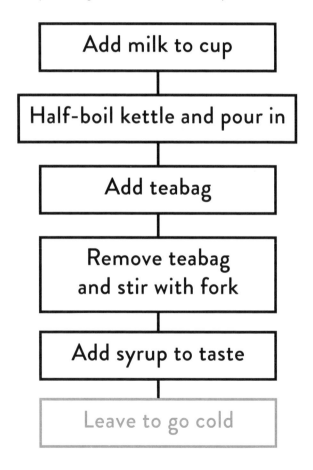

Add milk to cup

Half-boil kettle and pour in

Add teabag

Remove teabag
and stir with fork

Add syrup to taste

Leave to go cold

**Removing bad tea makers from the premises**

# Cup and saucer etiquette

A saucer is supposedly there to act as a coaster for the hot cup, but it is mostly used to rest a biscuit or two on. The saucer is not there to catch drips. How are you drinking tea? Like a thirsty bison? There should be **NO** drips to catch.

When using a cup with saucer there is no need to lift the saucer from the table. Let it stay on the table.

It can be tempting with a cup and saucer to hold the cup with your pinky finger pointed. Well, don't, it's frightfully uncouth! Unless you're a rule breaker? Then just do it to spite them!

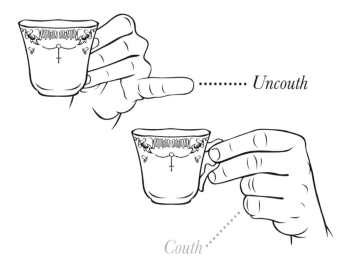

*Uncouth*

*Couth*

# DON'T DRINK FROM THE SAUCE

# Reheating tea

So you've let your tea go cold. At best you've felt the side of the cup and realised it's stone cold and at worst you've taken a deathly gulp of the cold fluids and instantly regretted everything.

What should you do?
The only thing you can do. Start again.

If you reheat tea you are destroying complex flavour molecules and further de-oxygenating the water, leading to a dull, lifeless brew. A cold cup of tea is good for only one thing and that is watering the plants.

Pop my brew in the microwave, will you?

**When you realise you're married to a savage**

## How to microwave tea

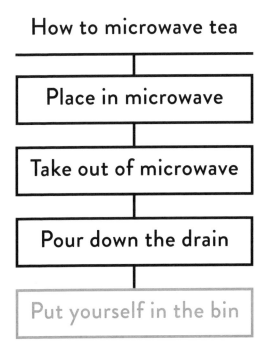

Place in microwave

Take out of microwave

Pour down the drain

Put yourself in the bin

# Types of tea

So many types for you to make incorrectly

## Taxonomy of tea

All the teas in and not in China:

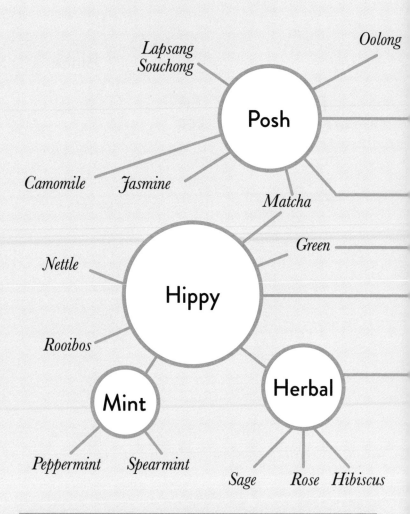

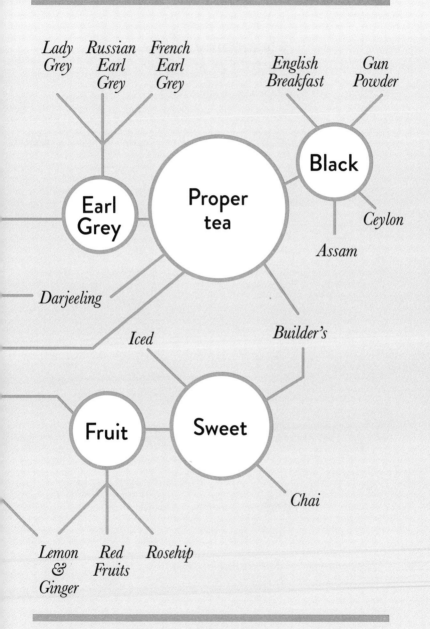

# Black tea

| Flavour | Method | Drinkers | Leaves | Strength |
|---------|--------|----------|--------|----------|
| Tea | Teapot/teabag | The entire world | Assam/Ceylon/Darjeeling | ★★★☆☆ |

Black teas are the common varieties of tea: Assam, Ceylon and Darjeeling. All are similar in production methods, although Darjeeling uses a tea bush with smaller leaves so is more delicate in flavour.

Of these Assam is by far the most common and the flavour we most associate with tea. Assam teas are sometimes sold as 'breakfast tea' and are often listed as an essential part of a cooked breakfast (alongside bacon and eggs) but by no means are these teas restricted to breakfast consumption. Be a rebel, have a breakfast tea at 9pm!

Sure, it's probably breakfast...

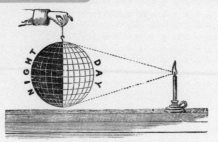

**Checking if it's time for breakfast tea**

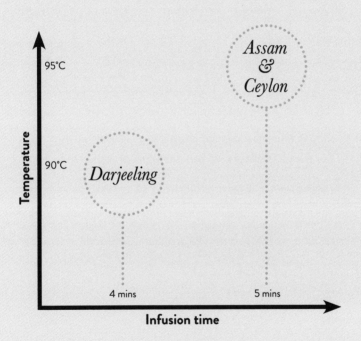

# Builder's

| Flavour | Method | Drinkers | Leaves | Strength |
|---------|--------|----------|--------|----------|
| Brick dust | In the mug | Labourers | Assam | ★★★★★ |

Builder's tea is an unusual brew as it can be made with one of many types of tea but has to be brewed in a specific way: very strong and very sweet.

Builder's tea is always made in a mug with a teabag
(never from a teapot and certainly never made with loose leaf tea).

The teabag is left to brew until it reaches 'Oompah loompah' orange.

Milk and ten sugars please, sweetheart

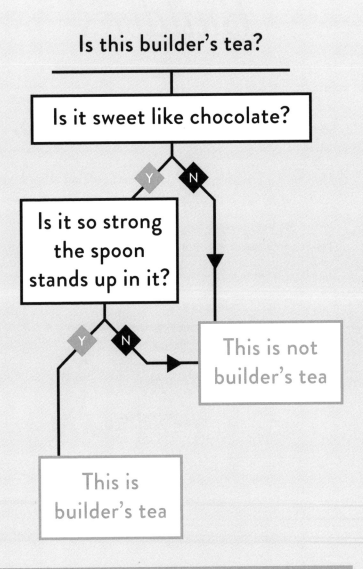

# Is this builder's tea?

**Is it sweet like chocolate?**

Y N

**Is it so strong the spoon stands up in it?**

Y N

This is not builder's tea

This is builder's tea

# Builder's brewing instructions

To make builder's tea, first boil a kettle and place a teabag
into a sturdy mug (preferably with a 'humorous' motif).
Dust off the paint and plaster from the mug, then pour in
boiling water. Leave your infusion to brew for a minimum
of four minutes and make small talk with your labourer.
If desired, stew. Add milk and plenty of sugar to taste.

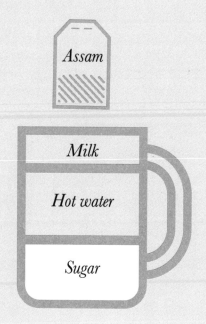

Builder's brews are essential for any DIY or manual tasks.
The more complex the job, the more tea is needed...

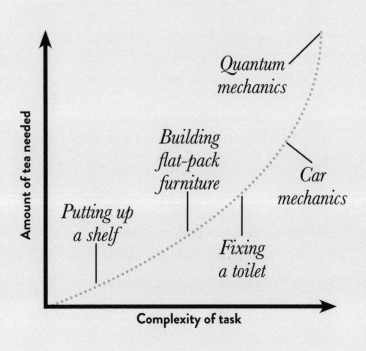

# *Earl Grey*

| Flavour | Method | Drinkers | Leaves | Strength |
|---------|--------|----------|--------|----------|
| Drawer liner | Teapot | Old ladies | Assam | ★★☆☆☆ |

Earl Grey is a tea that has been flavoured with the oil of the Bergamot Orange. Because of this orange flavour it is normally taken with a slice of lemon rather than milk. Loose leaves are preferred over a teabag, but if you must a teacup and teabag can be used.

**It is never served in a mug, you disgusting philistine!**

Earl Grey is named after, unsurprisingly, Earl Grey, who was supposedly gifted the blend in 1803 by a Chinese merchant.
Sounds like complete marketing codswallop.

It's not your tea. It's mine!

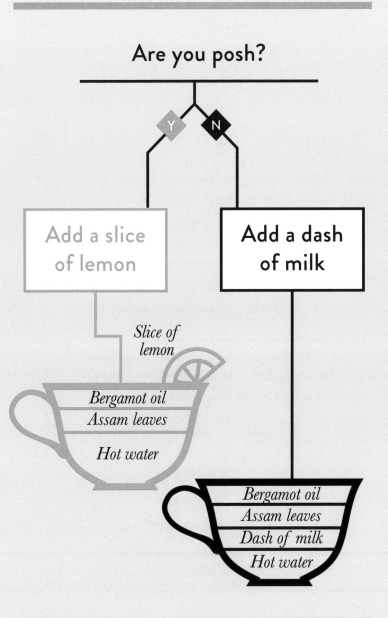

# Are you posh?

Y  N

Add a slice of lemon

Add a dash of milk

*Slice of lemon*

*Bergamot oil*
*Assam leaves*

*Hot water*

*Bergamot oil*
*Assam leaves*
*Dash of milk*
*Hot water*

# Can you have too much Earl Grey?

Yes, obviously you can.

The bergamot oil in Earl Grey has been found to be a mild irritant. There is a case of an Austrian man who had been drinking four litres of black tea every day with no ill-effects, so far so normal. He switched to drinking four litres of Earl Grey tea every day and after five weeks he began noticing muscle cramps and spasms.

In a move that surprised absolutely no one, he switched back to black tea and the symptoms almost instantly subsided. So there we have it, make sure you have no more than three litres of Earl Grey every day.

Fine, a barrel of tea was too much

# Earl Grey variations

| Cornflower |
| Earl Grey |
| Hot water |

**Lady Grey**

| Vanilla syrup |
| Steamed milk |
| Earl Grey |

**London Fog**

| Lemongrass |
| Earl Grey |
| Hot water |

**Russian Earl Grey**

| Rose petals |
| Earl Grey |
| Hot water |

**French Earl Grey**

# Gunpowder

| Flavour | Method | Drinkers | Leaves | Strength |
|---------|--------|----------|--------|----------|
| Singed bush | Teapot | Tea nerds | Assam | ★★★★☆ |

Rather than being actual gunpowder, you pranny, gunpowder tea is made with green tea that has been steamed and rolled into small pellets that resemble gunpowder pellets.

The flavour of gunpowder tea is fairly smokey so more suited to a tea aficionado rather than a casual drinker.

**When you've used actual gunpowder**

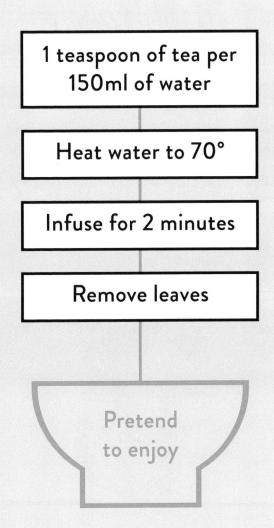

1 teaspoon of tea per 150ml of water

Heat water to 70°

Infuse for 2 minutes

Remove leaves

Pretend to enjoy

# *Oolong*

| Flavour | Method | Drinkers | Leaves | Strength |
|---------|--------|----------|--------|----------|
| ooOoooh! | Teapot | Hipsters | Green/black | ★★★★☆ |

Oolong tea is made in the same way as many black teas but the leaves are withered in the sun and are not allowed to oxidise fully so it falls somewhere between green and black tea.

Oolong is treated in the same way you would black tea with water at 90° and infused for 3 minutes, although it shouldn't be served with milk.

Oolong's finest quality is that the leaves can be steeped up to 3 times and each time you use them different flavour notes will appear.

**Green tea**

*Light and fruity*

*Oolong!*

**Black tea**

*Rich and complex*

# *Chai*

| Flavour | Method | Drinkers | Leaves | Strength |
|---------|--------|----------|--------|----------|
| Autumn/ Christmas | Saucepan | Hipsters | Black | ★☆☆☆☆ |

Chai tea, of late, has been perverted by the big c**fee chains into a Chai Latte, a drink so sweet and over-spiced it's like being force fed Christmas and Halloween at the same time.

'Proper' chai tea is a more nuanced affair of strong black tea, infused with spices and placed directly into the milk and sugar. Chai tea is not steeped in a teapot but simmered in a saucepan until well steamed. It goes without saying that Chai pairs especially well with biscuits.

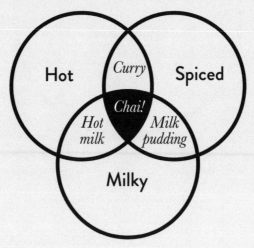

# Chai variations

Black tea
Spices*
Milk

**Masala Chai**

Sugar
Whipped cream

Black tea
Pumpkin spice
Syrup
Sugar, sweets & candy canes
Milk
Sweetener

**C\*\*fee chain
Chai Latte
abomination**

Black tea
Spices*
Lemon
Water

**Sulaimani Chai**

*\*Cardamom, ginger, cinnamon, cloves and nutmeg*

# Pu-erh

| Flavour | Method | Drinkers | Leaves | Strength |
|---------|--------|----------|--------|----------|
| Mud/kippers | Teapot | Aficionados | Black | ★★★★☆ |

Pu-erh tea is black tea that has been fermented with mould and bacteria and pressed into a cake shape, very much like a blue cheese. Also like blue cheese Pu-erh tea is an acquired taste.

There are two types of Pu-erh, raw and ripe. If you make it incorrectly ripe can taste like dirt and raw can taste like fish. Delicious!

So unless you like kipper tea, it is all the more important to follow infusion timings.

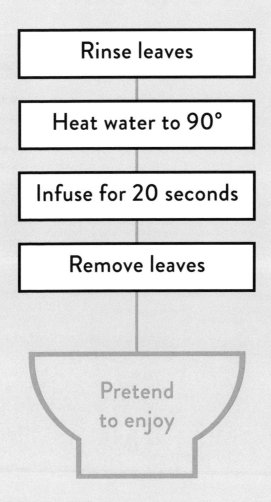

Rinse leaves

Heat water to 90°

Infuse for 20 seconds

Remove leaves

Pretend
to enjoy

# Cold brew

| Flavour | Method | Drinkers | Leaves | Strength |
|---------|--------|----------|--------|----------|
| Coldness | Glass jar | Hipsters | Black/ Green | ★☆☆☆☆ |

Cold-brew tea is as simple as it sounds. You place your leaves of choice in cold water and let it steep... slowly. Normally overnight. Brewing tea this way removes bitterness as the leaves have not been damaged by the heat of boiling water. The infusion is also lighter and sweeter. If you've found green tea too bitter, then the cold-brew process is an ideal way to remove that bitterness and leave a delicately flavoured tea.

*Slice of lemon*

*Sugar*

*Ice*

*Cold-brew tea*

**Iced tea**

# *Fruit*

| Flavour | Method | Drinkers | Leaves | Strength |
|---------|--------|----------|--------|----------|
| Nothing | Cup | Strawberry fools | Twigs and berries | ☆☆☆☆☆ |

Fruit teas are not real tea, they are merely tasteless
twigs and berries swished around in water.

They have supposed health benefits that can't be proven so are
not real medicine. They impart little to no flavour into the tea.
What is the point of fruit tea? Nobody knows.

**Fruit tea flavour profile**

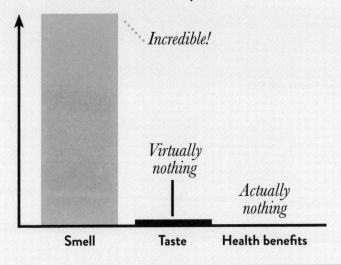

# *Herbal*

| Flavour | Method | Drinkers | Leaves | Strength |
|---------|--------|----------|--------|----------|
| Herby | Teapot | Hippies | Herbs | ★★☆☆☆ |

There are umpteen varieties of herbal teas on the market, with wild variations such as Sassafras and Sage, Skullcap and Sakurayu... well, that's just a small selection from the 'S' section. The list is vast.

The most common and flavoursome herbal teas are Camomile, Rooibos and Cannabis. Low in caffeine, with a soothing effect, Camomile and Rooibos teas are available everywhere. Cannabis tea on the other hand is illegal.

**This is NOT Sage**

# Mint

| Flavour | Method | Drinkers | Leaves | Strength |
|---------|--------|----------|--------|----------|
| Mint, duh! | Teapot | Moroccans | Mint/green | ★★☆☆☆ |

Mint tea is part of the herbal tea family, but it has a culture all of its own. Mint tea is synonymous with Morocco, where it is served after food to aid digestion and to cleanse the palate. Moroccan mint tea is traditionally poured from the teapot to a small cup from a large height. It's tremendous fun trying not to pour boiling water over your hands but it does serve a purpose: the height oxygenates the brew and adds a fresh flavour.

**Moroccan mint tea**

**Peppermint tea**

# *Lapsang Souchong*

| Flavour | Method | Drinkers | Leaves | Strength |
|---------|--------|----------|--------|----------|
| Ashtray | Teapot | Heavy smokers | Black | ★★★★★ |

Lapsang Souchong is a black tea made from the older, larger, less tender leaves, that have been smoked over a charcoal fire. The flavour is intense and not surprisingly full of smoke.

People who drink Lapsang Souchong are like those terrible bores who order the hottest curry on the menu, or drink those awful smokey whiskeys. Show offs, who pretend to like intense things so they will get your approval.

Oh, did I mention I drink Lapsang Souchong? I take it in my drawing room with all my trophies!

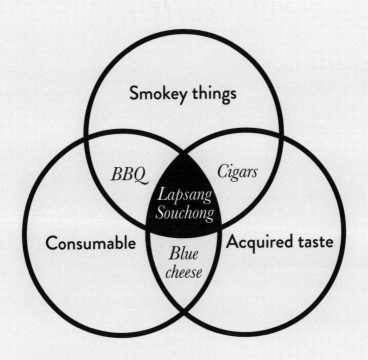

# White, green & yellow

| Flavour | Method | Drinkers | Leaves | Strength |
|---------|--------|----------|--------|----------|
| Not a lot | Teapot | Health nuts | Various | ★☆☆☆☆ |

White green and yellow teas are all to do with how oxidised the leaves have been in the production process. The more oxidation the darker the leaf. With more oxidation comes a stronger flavour. So subtlety is the name of the game here.

White tea is essentially just the tea bud with no oxidisation at all. It is withered in the sun before oxidisation can occur. Yellow teas are somewhere between green and oolong in flavour and oxidisation levels. They are also far less common because Yellow tea sounds like you might be getting a cup of hot urine.

Much like a cup of hot urine,
All of these teas are taken without milk.

# Caffeine content vs hipster-ness

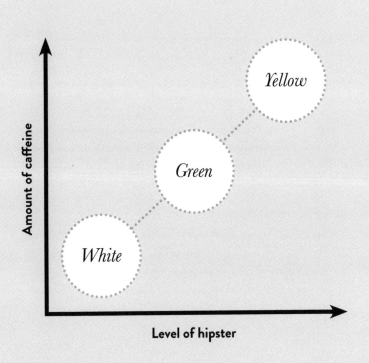

# Tea occasions

When and where to have tea?

# *Tea occasions*

Would you like a cup of tea? Of course you would.
Even if you don't want a cup of tea you should have a cup
of tea. A cup of tea solves everything and is good for you.
You should have a cup now...

# When is tea appropriate?

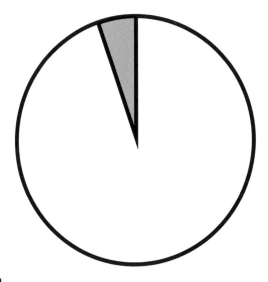

☐ **Always**

■ **Also always, but in brown**

# The first tea of the day

Upon waking there are 3 necessary functions one must perform: your morning evacuation, getting dressed and finally brewing a decent cup of tea.

Studies have shown that having a cuppa in the morning can increase concentration, lower your heart rate and make you a better lover [citation needed]. Fools have coffee for breakfast, champions drink tea.

## Did you drink tea this morning?

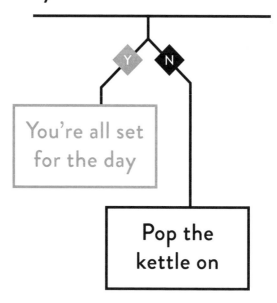

You're all set
for the day

**Pop the
kettle on**

**Before you've had your morning cuppa**

# Coping with disasters

If you're coping with a disaster you are probably in mild shock. To which a cup of hot, sweet tea is the perfect remedy:

### Sugar

No matter how big the disaster your body will be using adrenaline to cope. It's not to everyone's taste, but the sugar in the tea acts to replace this lost adrenaline.

### Heat

When in shock your body needs heat to counteract the chilling effects of shock. Wrap your hands around a nice hot mug of tea. It's the perfect comfort and gives you something tangible to grip on to.

### Hydration

Hydration is always important but after a shock or upset it is even more critical as your body starts to use resources more rapidly. Get glugging tea!

This is a 3 cups of tea problem!

# 99 problems? A cuppa solves them all

| Ailment | Solution |
|---|---|
| Personal emergency | Cup of tea |
| Family emergency | Pot of tea |
| Existential crisis | To know tea exists |
| Shock! | Cup of sweet tea |
| Bereavement | Tea and a biscuit |
| Nuclear winter | Iced tea |

# Tea cooling timeline

Glugging a mouthful of cold tea is the worst thing that has ever happened. A full mouthful of ice cold tea is doubly troubling because you know what it could have been. But alas you've let it go cold once again. It should go without saying that you never microwave cold tea, they don't even treat dogs like that.

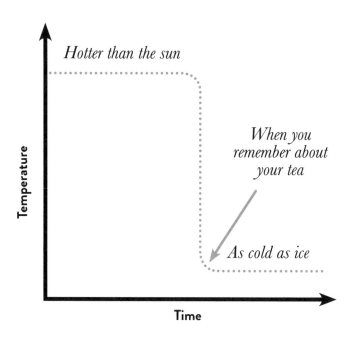

# Why your tea went cold at work

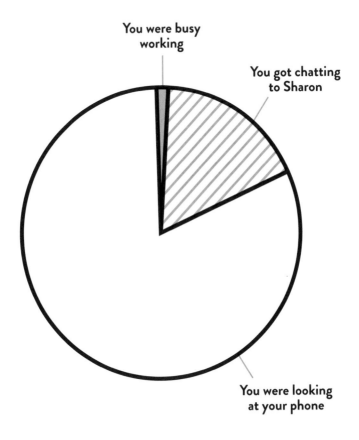

You were busy
working

You got chatting
to Sharon

You were looking
at your phone

# Drinking tea as a parent

Time is precious as a parent to a toddler or baby. Grabbing a moment between nappy changes and tantrums to sit and sip a refreshing cup of tea can be tricky. Which is why the experience can be so much sweeter when you finally manage to sneak off and enjoy five minutes of peace with a cup of tea and a biscuit without the little savages ruining it for you.

# How to drink tea as a parent

Have children

Make tea

Forget you made tea

Drink mouthful of cold tea

Resent having children

# Making tea in the office

Making a round of tea is a great way to ingratiate yourself in the office. Colleagues will take it in turn to offer to make tea for a select few tea-drinkers. It's all part of the social tapestry of the workplace.

There will be someone in every office who never makes the tea but always requests one. If you haven't made a tea in a while then know this: everyone in the office thinks that person is you!

**When you offer to make tea at just the wrong moment**

# YOU CAN'T SPELL TEAM WITHOUT TEA

Irritating office managers

# Tea with food

What to pair with tea and what to dunk

# *Tea with food*

Tea pairs particularly well with the finest of the food groups: biscuits, cakes, scones and sandwiches. These foods balance their flavours perfectly with a cup of tea. A sweet biscuit and a bitter Earl Grey? Or a crumbly scone with a vast vat of English breakfast? Made for each other.

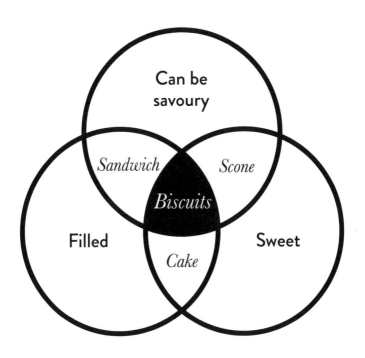

# Biscuits

Any cup of tea that has ever been served at any point in history would have been made better by simply adding a biscuit. There are no three words that have brought joy to so many as 'tea and biscuits'.

Two of mankind's greatest inventions brought together in one experience that you don't even have to count as a meal? Incredible.

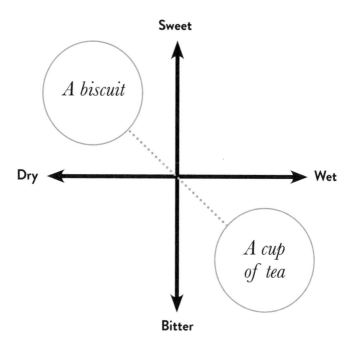

# Dunking chart

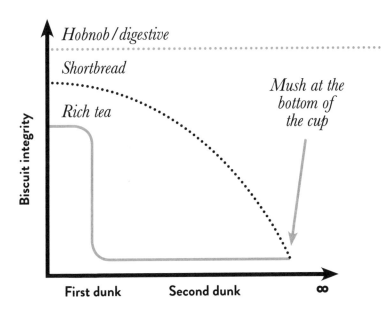

# Taxonomy of biscuits

Biscuits found in biscuit barrels, although not all are biscuits...

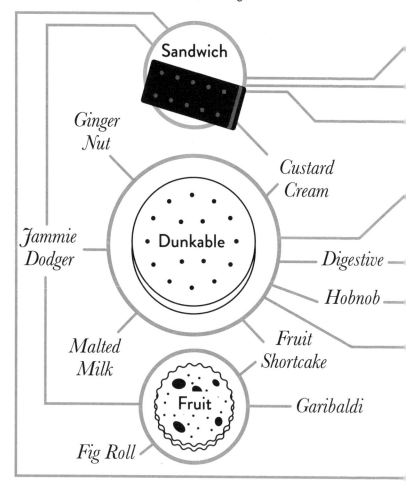

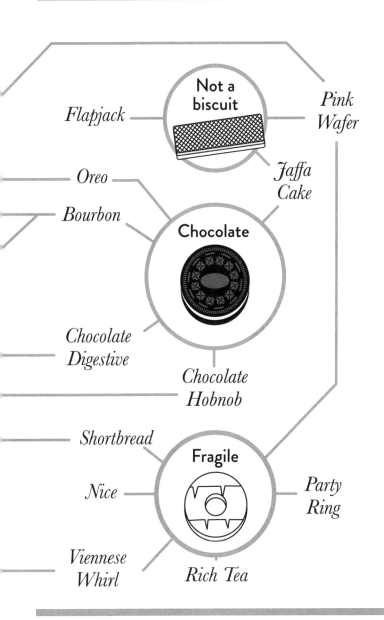

**Not a biscuit**

Flapjack

Pink Wafer

Oreo

Jaffa Cake

Bourbon

**Chocolate**

Chocolate Digestive

Chocolate Hobnob

Shortbread

**Fragile**

Nice

Party Ring

Viennese Whirl

Rich Tea

# Cake

What tea should you have with what cake?
One of life's tougher questions. The sweet and sometimes
floral notes in cake will match perfectly with an Oolong.

| Cake | Tea pairing |
|---|---|
| Victoria sponge | English Breakfast |
| Lemon Drizzle cake | Camomile |
| Battenberg | Green |
| Fruit cake | Earl Grey |
| Fish cake | Don't be silly |
| Chocolate cake | Peppermint/Fruit |
| Cream slice | Builder's |

It goes without saying that you
should never dunk cake.

# Is it a biscuit or a cake?

Defining if something is a cake or a biscuit can be confusing, especially with shortbread and shortcake! Cakes can be eaten with a fork, and biscuits can be eaten by holding them, but we've all seen people pick up cakes and eat them like a biscuit. Awful wretches.

The difference between a cake and a biscuit is rather simple. A cake will go hard when stale and a biscuit will become soft.

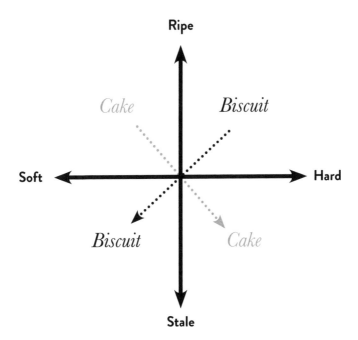

# Afternoon tea

Afternoon tea was essentially invented by Queen Victoria
and is the most inspired innovation of the 19th century,
a meal between meals!

It is served in the afternoon, obviously, and is a rather
delicate affair of cakes, cut sandwiches, biscuits and
scones, all served with a giant pot of tea.

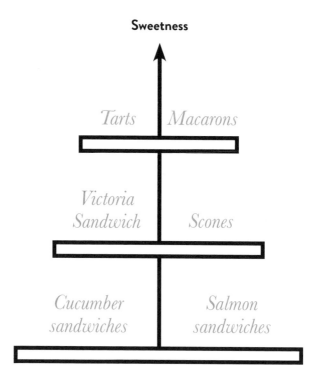

# Cream tea

A cream tea is very similar to afternoon tea in that it is served in the afternoon. But a cream tea consists solely of tea, scones, cream (preferably clotted) and jam.

When assembling your scone there are two schools of thought that originate from either Devon or Cornwall. One is clearly incorrect. As you can see from the below diagram, the 'jam first' route ensures that you receive the maximum amount of cream and is therefore the right way.

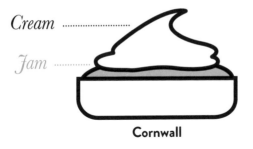

*Cream* ...................

*Jam* ...........

**Cornwall**

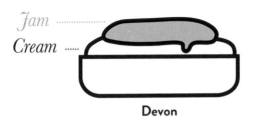

*Jam* .....................

*Cream* ......

**Devon**

# Tea and toast

Tea and toast is a quick, delicious breakfast but it's also a snack that can be enjoyed at any time of the day due to its supreme simplicity. Hot buttered toast and refreshing tea will always hit the spot.

Tea and toast is so popular that there are several hipster pop-up cafés in that there London devoted entirely to the combination. Of course there are, they will do anything in that there London.

Roll up, roll up, jam on toast, only £15

# Toppings for toast

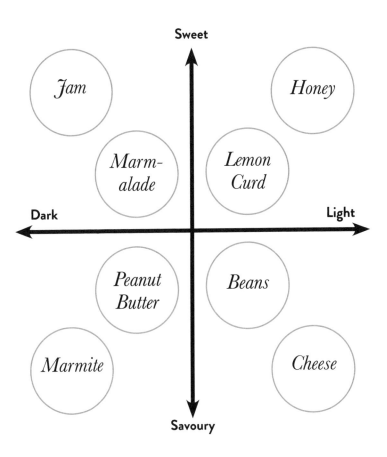

# Tea in cooking

Tea can be used in a myriad of ways in cooking,
as it is a herb and it can be treated as such.

Freshly brewed tea works well as a stock for
cooking rice or as a base for a noodle broth.

Tea smoke, made by burning tea leaves, is a classic Chinese
way to impart flavour into meat and fish.

If you are going to experiment with tea in cooking,
please find a recipe. Don't try out your new tea-trifle
on unsuspecting guests at your next soirée.
It will be awful and you'll never live it down.

I do hope you all enjoy my fishy tea balls!

# Easy tea loaf recipe

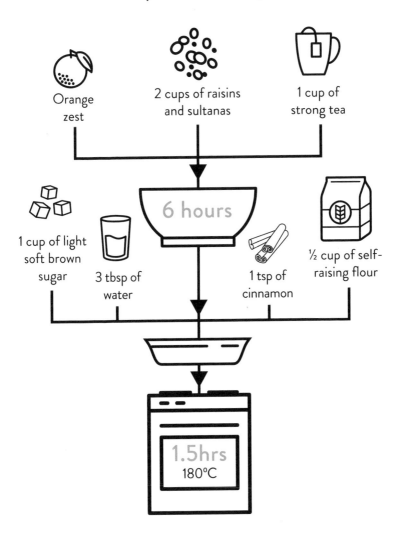

Orange
zest

2 cups of raisins
and sultanas

1 cup of
strong tea

6 hours

1 cup of light
soft brown
sugar

3 tbsp of
water

1 tsp of
cinnamon

½ cup of self-
raising flour

1.5hrs
180°C

# About the author

Stephen Wildish is the author of *How to Give Zero F\*cks*, *How to Vegan*, *How to Swear* and *How to Adult*. He secretly likes drinking c\*\*fee.

Stephen is the current 100m and 200m sack-race world-record holder.

With thanks to George Orwell.

Pop Press, an imprint of Ebury Publishing
20 Vauxhall Bridge Road
London SW1V 2SA

Pop Press is part of the Penguin Random House group of companies whose
addresses can be found at global.penguinrandomhouse.com

Copyright © Stephen Wildish 2020
Illustration on page 25 © Apic/Contributor/Gettyimages

Stephen Wildish has asserted his right to be identified as the author of this
Work in accordance with the Copyright, Designs and Patents Act 1988

First published by Pop Press in 2020

www.penguin.co.uk

A CIP catalogue record for this book is available from the British Library

ISBN 9781529107562

Printed and bound by TBB, a.s. Slovakia

Penguin Random House is committed to a
sustainable future for our business, our readers
and our planet. This book is made from Forest
Stewardship Council® certified paper.